SKY AND THE FLOWERS

Sandhya Balakrishnan

BookLeaf
Publishing

India | USA | UK

Presentation by *BookLeaf Publishing*

Web: www.bookleafpub.com

E-mail: info@bookleafpub.com

ISBN: 9789363318441

First edition 2024

To my Mother

ACKNOWLEDGEMENT

my sincere thanks to the green leaf publications for bringing out this book.

NUMB TO BEAUTY

Even in the most
challenging situations
the tenderness,
wonder and joy
that flowers
evoke in us
can't be undone;

if only
one looked at them!

WHAT IF

In a swirl
the kaleidoscope
cooked up a magic.
Arranged
bits of rainbow
to paint a graphic.
Beauty reveals - not
the underlying logic.
A pattern
extraordinary,
an experience unique!

Had
the kaleidoscope
picked up
an alternate magic?
Re-arranged pieces
to paint a graphic –
surely
a beauty distinct,
yet
another logic.
A pattern
extraordinary,
the experience unique!

TAKEN BY GRATITUDE

3

She arrives unawares
and all must change!
Pettiness in me flees,
all I perceive is grace.

A sweetness descends,
love floods my heart.
Gratitude is here!
I'm renewed in her subtle art.

A POINT TO ETERNITY

"Is it possible?"
I thought,
for I had collapsed
into a point.
I crumbled down further,
right into the center;
I was reduced to a nought!

A compressed eternity - dark and deep
stillness presided;
Stay!
I was persuaded.
Ensnared
in an everlasting
stupor,
time and mind
ceased to wander.

When,
unexpectedly a whisper
"Where am I!"
shattered the silence,
kindled in me
a will to fly!
Out of the chasm

I blossomed 'n' bloomed,
whereupon
I found myself on the bed
in layers cocooned.

"What an unusual dream!"
I woke up with a start!
and looked around bewildered – I had
come away from the point!

SKETCHING WOES

6

"Am I here
or there?",
asked the line crossly.
"Do I belong
in this space
or that?"

"Nowhere!
you're born anew
in the mind's eye,
and gone too soon
in a blink",
mumbled the artist.

YELLOW TREE

On a mundane day
travelling on a bus,
I saw a
blooming yellow tree.
She danced
with her ochre boughs,
the wind played along
with glee.

I gazed
at the scene
with all my being;
alive
to this celestial show!
While I
disappeared,
just lingered
the feeling
"I'm the joyous tree
with a golden glow!"

With a blaring sound,
the cold fate
resolved to move
the window!

MOM

8

It's hard to imagine
my mom as a girl
who dreamt
a million dreams.

Now my dreams are
her dreams!

SPIRIT OF FRIENDSHIP

From nothingness
blossomed an energy;
Not planned, nor planted -
It chose the time,
picked the ground,
everything came together
quite unknown.

Growing
in its own pace,
unaware of morrow
brought colorful moods:
Love, anger, joy and sorrow.

Without a form, we
barely sensed it.
In togetherness, we
truly experienced it.
It broke our walls,
set us free. We
reveled in its presence
spreading hope and cheer.

Was the spirit
because of us,

or just a
happy occurrence,
no one knew.
Was it alive?
Or did it
make us alive
is a question too.

As we moved
away,
out the energy spread -
into nothingness
it disappeared.

Never to bloom the same again
it left us with a heartache!

MEETING SIMPLICITY

If I ever meet
"Simplicity",
I would
inquire of her -
The secret
to her charm and
the silent power.

She hides
nothing, yet
deeply mysterious,
her presence
never screams
and is quite gracious.

Perfectly content
and happy
in her hue
she's unassuming
yet touches
your very soul!

Homecoming

Step out
of your home,
to enter
your real home.

Place your barefoot
on the ground.
Feel
the loving touch, when
she leans to kiss
your tiny feet -
Mother's happy
to have you home.

Gaze
at the ethereal roof,
watch
the noise go down.
Eyes may fail
to see the ends,
heart holds
the boundless.
Drop the worries,
soar up
in space,

in Father's
almighty embrace.

Softly tread,
walk some steps,
explore a maze of
color 'n shapes.
No walls are
raised
to hold you down
in one and only
dwelling place.
Where all's thriving 'n growing:
people, trees, animal, birds –
all your kith and kin.

MASTER ARTIST

Whisper your truth,
sweet blossoms!
Who colors so deep
thy soul?
Beyond
the narrow reasoning
of science
and the mere exaggeration
of art -
Whisper
your truth ,
only the truth!
Who colors so deep
thy soul?

A PLACE I LONG TO GO

has no name,
in need of fame,
no map
ever made,
roads
neither paved -
A place I long to go.

None can reach
at will,
no magical words
to spill,
wasted paper bills -
A place I long to go

An elusive space,
here time
stands still.
One enters
by Grace,
not mortal skill! -
A place I long to go

The World
or "I"

can't stain this place;
As one alights
all is ceased,
back again
as the spell
is breached.

GREED

A whole generation
is plagued
by a syndrome,
of digging into reserves
to the very last
and moving
to the next
sure as fast;
won't stop,
not even pause –
to think
what this disease
is gonna cost!

Earth is free!
air, water at large
free to use,
right to abuse.
As long as needs are
met today
greedy wants are
comforted away!
Won't stop,
not even pause –
to think
what this disease
is gonna cost!

God made roof

I love to watch the God made roof,
it amuses me, even when I'm blue.
The splash of colors bring different moods,
The divine's art is what I look forward to.

When the fluffy cotton candies drift,
surprisingly all my thoughts shift.
when a flock of birds make a flying V,
I want to tag along - make a Y from V.

Drear n fear run from the golden ball of fire,
see the world glow - it's the coolest chandelier.
that's not all, there's a charming silver ball,
with an array of star lights, at a dance ball.

Ever heard of a roof that roars and explodes?
Well, this one does with lighting effects.
After the outburst it tends to tear up
happy or sad, sure will soak you up!

A PURPOSEFUL LIFE

What's my life's purpose?
Am I doing fine?
What if I never found out?
What if I waste this life?
Why do I need to know?

While caught in this thought storm,
a tiny bird flies past me chirping incessantly.

Ah! It's a beautiful day!
Thank God for the sweet joys of life!

If I'm here for a purpose,
the purpose will be met,
no matter what!

JUST BE

20

If it weren't for the language,
I know that I would just be.

I'M NOT MYSELF

I don't wanna get up, I don't wanna move
I don't wanna meet the world!
I'm lost, blank, not happy not sad -
can't feel anything, I'm a rock.
I'm a shirt, turned inside out and
don't care if I'm not
straightened out.
Oh God! I'm not myself today
From me, I'm quite far away!
How do I go back?
Where do I start?
Climb up or hop down?
Walk some distance too
So many bridges and overflies -
none connect me to ME,
none can take me home.

GIFT FOR A CHILD

To see the dancing fields stretched to the
horizon,
to hear the chirping birds n soft gushing streams,
to walk on velvety green, soak the clean fresh
air,
to get a whiff of scented flowers, soil the hands
with clay.
I wish these gifts for every child - today and
forever;

And yet we changed the world for the better!

FEW PRECIOUS MOMENTS

Few precious moments
come alive
when the heart is open,
mind is still,
and the invisible
comes out to play.

Hold the space,
watch it work
in a thousand
miraculous ways.

Don't let
the mind
wander or probe -
lest you push
the force away.

A FIST OF EARTH

Mounds of gold can't satisfy
a man's heart,
as much as a fist of earth
can satisfy that of a child.

BEING A FLOWER

25

O joyous blossoms!

The tenderness,
purity,
humility,
sincerity and courage
you reveal
is of another world.